The
Huntress

For Brian

Also by Pascale Petit

Icefall Climbing

Heart of a Deer

Tying the Song (Co-edited with Mimi Khalvati)

The Zoo Father

El Padre Zoológico/The Zoo Father

The Wounded Deer

The Huntress

Pascale Petit

seren

Seren is the book imprint of
Poetry Wales Press Ltd
Nolton Street, Bridgend, Wales, CF31 3BN
www.seren-books.com

ISBN 1-85411-396-8

A CIP record for this title is available from the British Library.

The publisher acknowledges the financial assistance
of the Welsh Books Council.

Printed by Bell & Bain, Glasgow.

Cover painting: Animal Tales 1 by Franz Marc.

Back cover portrait of the author by Brian Fraser.

CONTENTS

Three Horses

Come in. Come in, and see
what no-one has witnessed.
You step in and you're outside.
So outside. There are no humans,
just three horses in a field,
the sky pressing against your forehead,
urging you to acknowledge
something is wrong. Three horses.
Two foals drink from a trough
and are normal. You recognise your brother.
You must look now at the big palomino mare,
at her face which is twice the size it should be.
You walk up, just as I used to walk in,
closing the front door behind me.
Every molecule in the room
told my eyes to look away
but a daughter must meet her mother's gaze.
Those bulging hazel eyes weeping blood –
inhuman, beyond the animal.
A daughter must put out her hand
and touch her mother's muzzle –
huge and red-brown, against
the open field of the carpet.
No firm bone under the creased flesh,
as if her body is being digested
from the inside. Her breath comes hard.
Run your fingers along the furrows
and find the straps of the halter
buried in the bag of her neck.
Do what was required of me,
what I did not know how to do –
cut her free. See, just above
her nostrils, the two punctures
of a rattlesnake's fangs.
She'll hobble to the trough
and recover. You'll be allowed
to leave, you'll be released.

The Snake House

It's time to go up to your front door, Mother,
and ring the rattling buzzer of a bell,
the door with two curved fangs.
I go in, into the muscular throat of the hall,
down the tunnel that's closing now
to a pinpoint of light.
I'm in the swallowing living-room,
washing it for you, half-alive,
like a man preparing for the rain-dance
in the dry arroyo. He reaches
into the pit and washes the snakes
so that later when he dances with the 'little mothers'
in his mouth, they won't bite.
I'm a child playing in the pen
with my pet rattlers,
giving them bread and milk.
As long as I'm unscared
they won't strike. And you're saying,
"Only a girl-child can do this".
My cheeks are almost seamless now,
countless grafts hide the necrosis.

The Summoner

"But we never see you" my brother shouts,
as if she's there with him – our divine mother –
and her home is Kukulcan's shrine.
The air fills with fever feathers,
her eyes blue quetzal eggs
that split open like rattlesnake pupils.
The rain hisses its warning,
the green-lightning bird strikes.
Oh the spirals I've drawn counterclockwise
to uncoil her power.
The diamondbacks I've caught and eaten raw.
I have eaten a snake's heart
to let light into my heart.
I have come back with serpent stealth
singing my snake songs, older and strong.
I have sacrificed my life to the rattler-god.
But my brother still stands in her granny flat,
among her sacks of soiled nighties,
her lithium pill dispenser,
her last lipstick-smeared fag, its ash.
And her unmade bed behind him.
Where if I search long enough
with my viper's heat-sensors,
I will find what I came for –
the snake head that even decapitated
will still have the reflex to bite me.

The Den

In the silence of my own home
I hear the buzz like a shivering of icy leaves.
The back of my neck tickles
and I glimpse the rattler's tail
disappearing under the floorboards,
its skin faded as old documents.
And I lift the boards
while still sitting in my chair.
The nails pop out as if with a claw-hammer.
Then I see the den my visitor
keeps returning to –
hundreds of ancestor-snakes
hibernating. I don't move
in case one feels the vibration
and wakes the others.
I don't want them roused like a beehive.
I wait calmly, then blink once –
that's all I allow myself.
Just as when I sat with you Mother,
I let my ophidian mask
slip down my face
and blinked no more, its eyes lidless.
I don't let my forked black tongue
taste the air for wind jewels
of your scent, three years after your death.
I look through the renailed floorboards
and see our letters rolled tight
where I have hidden them,
a bolus of papers
seeking warmth from each other,
scrolled like ancient codices.
Each letter sleeping with its venom
tucked in the fold.

Portrait of My Mother as Xipe Totec

When she said she was Xipe Totec,
Aztec god of springtime, I believed her.
Sitting me down opposite her rocking-chair
she explained what that meant:
she needed to flay my skin
and dance in it in the sunshine.
We had no net curtains then,
the neighbours always looked in
when she turned on the lights.
There was no TV, just her face
which shone like a screen
I couldn't help watching
but wished would break down.
I wondered whether the people passing
saw how she possessed me, and if
I would ever stop shivering
as if I'd been skinned. My hands
hung from her wrists like mittens.
My tongue, behind her lips,
asked her how she was feeling.
"Better" she smiled, "now that the seeds
are sprouting in the fields."
She walked out of the front door.
And I found myself dancing alone on the lawn –
a hollow sheath, golden, shot with green.

House of Darkness

Silver bells painted on my cheeks
so Mother could always find me,
my hair cut, woven into hers.
I polished the obsidian floor.
The sweetness at the centre
belonged to Tezcatlipoca –
Aztec Smoking-Mirror god.
Mother's memories rose
and sank into the burnished tiles.
Sometimes a vision serpent swayed
and a jaguar reared from its jaws.
Jimson weed takes away terror,
but at dawn before Mother woke,
I obediently dusted the dresser –
drawers full of stingray spines,
swordfish beaks, and a blade
called the Perforator
"for piercing tongues of daughters who talk".

The Rattlesnake Mother

Her skin sprouted emerald feathers.
She claimed she was Quetzalcoatl –
the plumed serpent,
needed hearts sacrificed to her
to get through the night.
At first, her bird half was a quetzal –
her chair a mist-draped forest,
a changing-cubicle where
she kept trying on selves like clothes.
Had we opened the cloud-door
we'd have seen the bird's sudden beak,
our mother cowering in the corner, eyeless,
as a mockingbird kept dive-bombing her.
Then we'd hear a growl and know
her dog double had arrived
to escort her to hell,
and we'd have to follow. Just as a dog
will grab a rattler by the neck
and shake it until every bone
in its spine is broken,
so she attacked herself. We did nothing,
as if we were the dog's owners
and it was protecting us,
gnawing off her head,
tearing off strips of skin
until the intestines lay
flailing on our carpet –
great loops that gradually quietened.
When dawn came I held out my hand
and touched them.
They gave a last twitch
as if trying to recoil from me.
I think now how hard it was for her
to be a rattlesnake, how hated she was
by all the animal kingdom.

Her Mouse Daughter

I fidget with the serviette so as not to see
Mother's fingers change into snakes,

her pupils narrow to vertical slits
and the room suddenly darken. And the stars come out.

I watch them through our kitchen window,
waking in their crystal lairs.

I place my hands each side of my plate
according to her strict etiquette.

And while I wait to be excused,
I shrink into the smallest animal.

I even try to be what she says I am –
a mouse fed live into her cage.

But when she's stuffed with medication
like a snake that's swallowed a rat,

I run onto her nape
and with my tiny incisors I snip her spine.

My Mother's Mirror

Your make-up mirror
has a milky blue cast over it
like the eye of a snake
preparing to moult.
I am standing naked in your room
and you're painting me blue.
I don't know how I got here
or why your face shimmers
like a mirage through the Gitane haze
as you fasten copper bells around my neck,
teeth bracelets around my wrists.
You lead me to your dressing-table
which is two steps away
but seems far off as Chichén Itzá.
When you push my face into something cold –
I know it's just a small round make-up mirror,
not the Well of Sacrifice.
But when you tip it magnifying-side up –
jaws unlock
like a snake swallowing our house.
Into your mirror I fall,
down the long body of the Well,
past limestone shelves
ridged like a serpent's spine,
right into the rattler,
the tail-cone at the bottom,
the silver sludge of the glass,
where I lie
for what feels like a thousand years.

I surface in the glare of a Mayan forest.
Archaeologists pull me
out of the stinking waters.
They reconstruct my last day
from fragments of painted ceramic jars,

bracelets of teeth,
copper death-bells
and a carved stag antler
I might have bought in the market
before I came home to find the god waiting.
They say I was proud
to be chosen by the plumed serpent.
I arched my back over the rock
and let the priest knock out my teeth
for the next child's costume.
Through the red mist
that flowed from my mouth over my eyes,
I must have blinked twice
after the gold-plated knife
was plunged in my chest.
I must have seen my heart
raised up to the sky.

The Feast

I go back to the eve
of my eighteenth birthday,
open the grey curtains
and let moonlight flood in
as I unscrew the mirror.
It's thin and narrow
as a silent girl
who never leaves her room,
only four feet tall
and shakes as I lay it
flat on my bed.
I wait until it's smooth
as a silver picnic cloth
on a white altar,
then unfasten my rucksack,
bring out my treasures.
There's the silky bag
of a saturnian cocoon to slit,
nine fat moth larvae
to place on bare glass.
And a stone box
from the Temple of Butterflies,
containing nine monarchs
clinging to oyamel twigs.
While they're still numb
from the cold of my long journey,
I remove their orange wings,
arrange their brown bodies
on lace leaves.
Then I kneel on my pillow
and pray to Xochiquetzal –
Aztec butterfly goddess,
and to Itzpapalotl –
her moth double, Butterfly of Knives.
And I eat each offering.
I eat until the bitter flavours
of nitre and milkweed fade.

After the Washing-Up

A few moments ago, you called me.
Now my hands are plunged in molten magma.

But I come out of the kitchen
to brave you, Mother –

with that firecloud around your face
like a volcano that's just erupted,

your skin all wrinkled like lava.
That tight smile, as if you're tunnelling into the sun.

I need lead armour to get through this.
But we carry on sitting in your living-room

like the last family on earth,
our thoughts sandblasting the window,

no sound reaching us from the upper world.

Portrait of My Mother as Coatlicue

Like Cortés, I found her monstrous
and would have preferred
to bury her in the cathedral crypt.
But she was my mother,
as much a victim as a devourer.
When I reached puberty
and I moved into her house,
and for five years dusted
the skull rack and the flint knives,
and sat on her bed while she showed me
scenes from her previous life
carved into the soles of her feet,
and the scars seeping blue-green blood
that proved she was divine –
I never touched her basalt breast
or kissed her serpent lips.

Visit of the Were-Deer

My mother sits at her triple mirror
   holding a cigarette, but it's the mirrors
    that smoke. As she makes herself up
in black glass, she's Itzpapalotl from the Codex Borgia.
The side panels tremble like newborn wings
   of the Aztec moth goddess whose every scale
is a knife. Obsidian sparks sting her shoulders.
Her hands shake like volcano rabbits
   so that I will come and rescue her.

I have been hiding in the Sierra Madre
   to hunt peyote and dream my yarn paintings.
   They have a hole in the centre called the 'mirror'
for the soul to travel through. I, who can only approach
   in the form of a were-deer, squeeze myself through the gate
    in the central panel, thin as a Gitane, my antlers
rolled like a collapsed galaxy, my fur
   flickering with flame jets. I, the little doe,
    come like a breath to my mother's mouth.

My Mother's Wings

Then the mirrors clear and she's Xochiquetzal
  in her Butterfly Palace, her face new
    as the ever-young Toltec goddess.
The air in the glass panels has that sheen
  when she ascended the oyamel groves in her mother's arms
    just as the monarchs swarmed, coming in to roost.
That ripping sound rhythmic as surf
  was the sky's heartbeat whooshing in her ears.
She knew then to be unafraid
while the mariposas poured over her,
  her baby head caressed by exhausted wings.
    They even crawled over her eyes and tongue.

And now, as she tries to steady the lipstick,
  one emerges from her mouth. It tastes bitter
    to go back that far, to when she was left out
winter evenings in her pram "to harden".
  So long she has climbed, to sit in the sanctuary
    of her bedroom at the triple looking-glass –
a calm before the mania hits. Before
  the mirror layers peel back to her fossil self
    and she's a billion-year-old butterfly
breaking her rock chrysalis.
  Then lift-off, and she's a mile high
    even though her wings are boiling glass.

Portrait of My Brother as an Endurance Runner

Now that I know the secrets
of the Tarahumara tribe
famous for their long-distance races,
I urge my brother not to eat
Mother's fatty meals. Instead
I feed him rabbits, deer, rats.
Then mix the blood of a turtle
with the blood of a bat
and roll it with tobacco
into a cigar for him to smoke.
I dress him in loose clothes,
dry the head of an eagle
for a charm around his neck,
hang deer-hoof rattles from his waist.
Before Mother stirs, he sets out
at a steady pace, not fast
at first, but never slowing,
until he's run forty miles
in six hours. And so he continues,
the rattlers keep him awake.
Strips of mountain lion skin
protect his ankles.
When night falls, torches
of resinous pinewood are lit
and held by strangers
along the steep forest path.
He keeps on running until
he's old enough to realise
it's better to live in a cave
up a deep canyon alone
than to stay in his mother's house.

The Mantis Mother

When she says my brother will never
love another woman like her –
I see the praying mantis.
I look at Mother's face
the moment it changes –
that gold sheen it gets
in church before communion.
Her eyes green and bulging,
cold black dots at their centres,
her mouth a triangular point
worked by mandibles.
She is rocking herself
as she always does before a strike,
hypnotising her prey.
He must come to her,
her little Son, he is her Jesus.
I can see the spikes on her prayer-arms.
He believes she is religious.
He is still singing her praises
even as she snaps off his face
like a mask and chews it.
The long gloves of his arms
lie discarded on her pillow,
his body still pumping
mechanically into her.
She cleans her serrated forelegs
with her tongue, then folds
them back like jack knives
against their handles. And for a while
there is peace in our house.

The Mineral Mother

Your face has the violet luminescence
of the long dead.
Night after night I dreamt of this descent
until I reached the basalt door
where you wait to greet me,
your irises streaked like falcon's eye gems.
You lead me into the crystal crypts
that form in magma over time,
down smoky quartz rooms
where you live now,
your rock crystal skull
shot with tourmaline needles.
Your veins are fire opal.
I have come with my hammer and chisel
to break you up into jewels
that I can bring back to the surface.

The Children's Asylum

The nuns are talking
but she can't understand what they say.
She feels far away, in this ward
where all the beds are tilted upright,
are too tall, are trees.
Long thin girls are sleeping in them,
wearing leaf-nightdresses,
listening to the birds in their pillows.
Her own bed is a tree,
the sheets are rough as bark.
Like a tree she has no legs, no arms.
Her dreams are breaking out of their nests,
are chicks with open beaks
and orange winglets tangled
in branches with blue echoes
that soon grow into a thick wood
around her face – a madwood
in which there are trees that are beds that are girls
that are all her.
And none of them can speak. Matron leans over
my nine-year-old mother
in a white habit woven from silence.

A Cure

One pouring night, the nuns led
my nine-year-old mother

out of the children's asylum,
down to the water's edge

to the toads mating by moonlight.
They filled a shawl

with the singing toads
and wrapped it around her body,

rolled her tight along the bank
until the poison in their skins

shocked the jism out of her.

My Mother's Tongue

I have twisted a lightning bolt
into a spiral and eaten it.
From my stomach it gives orders.
I, who was never hugged by you,
or hugged you, Mother,
must lie on your corpse
feet to feet, breasts to breasts,
mouth to mouth.
I cannot help the words I am speaking
but say them without pause
in the language of your "angel".
I give you my body to eat,
my blood to drink,
my flesh for clothes.
I give you my breath.
You struggle and I wrestle with you
as you rise from the floor.
Now your black and shrivelled tongue
is hanging out of your mouth
and I must seize it and tear it out.
Then you fall down. The door opens.
And I leave, holding your tongue
in my cupped hands like a bird
that must be saved,
its wing-bones and spine
curled like an embryo.
I go out into the great field
and set it free.

The Witch Bottle

Mother – I have counted to a hundred
in the dark cellar, it's time to switch
on the light and open the door.
You have locked me in
like a foetus in formaldehyde.

        And now it's your turn:
I've gone back to the brewery
where you worked as I was forming –
glass exploding in the bottling machine
is how the world first sang to me.
I've picked an old brown beer bottle
and taken it to the sea to cleanse it,
then charged it with the light of the full moon.

Inside it I place one of your eyelashes,
your nail clippings, broken mirror, thorns,
a photo of you cut into a heart
stuck with nine rusty bent pins.
I fill this vessel with my urine.
Wind your red hair round the cork
and seal it with black wax.
                Then call.
You come to my door in agony,
begging to be released.
But I have buried my witch bottle
in the earth floor of my cellar inverted.
And it's my name scratched on the label.

The Singing Bowl

I hum "Mama" over and over
    until the water dances in my copper bowl.

I know how to rub the handles
    so the water rises like a fountain.

When I start my hands sting, like that time
    I closed my fist around a wasp,

just after I'd learnt to say my name.
    I shouted it to the long steep garden

of the children's home. To the silence
    like the wind across the Tibetan plateau.

I took the bowl you gave me and stared at it
    until it was you. Until the other parents

pulled away in their cars and the drive
    was quiet. And the children were asleep.

I lay on my bed, the poultice cold on my chest.
    The air was dull and grey. In my fever

the copper gleamed like a meteor. The Yogi
    forges his singing bowl from meteorite iron

which has barely burnt up through the thin atmosphere.
    I held your gift until the stinging passed.

Until my forearms were flutes, my femurs, trumpets.
    And the bowl was your skull. Five fountains

rose in star-formation. On the water
    I wrote my name in words of clear light.

Mother of Pearl

I have dressed in white to scare off sharks,
fastened a stone sinker round my ankle,
stopped up my ears and nose with wax.
Down the blue hospital corridors
I dive. The ward doors are heavy,
as if holding back a tide, which almost
knocks me over as I land at your bed.
Other patients and their visitors
cannot see what you are doing, Mother,
even though you are asleep, the silver lips
of your oyster mouth sealed, your hair
swaying like an undersea fire. Sunlight
plays moiré music on the ceiling
which I alone can interpret. Six minutes
I have held my breath. I developed
these lungs to survive in your element –
your daughter the deep-sea pearler.
A cord connects me to the surface,
but I will not tug on it yet. Six years
since you died, and still I dream myself back
to our last silent battle, my chest
imploding under the pressure. Soon,
you'll wake, and I'll claim my prize.

My Mother's Perfume

Strange how her perfume used to arrive long before she did,
    a jade cloud that sent me hurrying
first to the loo, then to an upstairs window to watch for her taxi.
    I'd prepare myself
by trying to remember her face, without feeling afraid. As she drew
    nearer I'd get braver
until her scent got so strong I could taste the coins in the bottom
    of her handbag.
And here I am forty years on, still half-expecting her. Though now
    I just have to open
the stopper of an expensive French bottle, daring only a whiff of
    Shalimar
which Jacques Guerlain created from the vanilla orchid vine.
    Her ghostly face
might shiver like Christ's on Veronica's veil – a green-gold blossom
    that sends me back
to the first day of the school holidays, the way I used to practise
    kissing her cheek
by kissing the glass. My eyes scanned the long road for a speck
    while the air turned amber.
Even now, the scent of vanilla stings like a cane. But I can also smell
    roses and jasmine
in the bottle's top notes, my legs wading through the fragrant path,
    to the gloved hand emerging
from a black taxi at the gate of Grandmother's garden. And for a
    moment I think I am safe.
Then Maman turns to me with a smile like a dropped
    perfume bottle, her essence spilt.

The Ghost Orchid

Eye level with her blue-white face,
I fall into the green throat at the centre,
down silk corridors to a hushed ward
where I'm back at Mother's bedside.
She whispers to me through closed lips
the texture of ghost orchids.
                                    Her last breath
drifts out into the cool swamp air
of the Fakahatchee night,
draws billowing hieroglyphs
to summon the great sphinx moth –
who appears like a god
hovering in front of the bloom,
his wings a thunderous whirr.
He uncoils his six-inch tongue.
It arches out slow-motion, then darts
into the ghost's long narrow nectary –
as if my mother is having all her words sucked out.

When I Talk With My Mother

She will pull me into her grave, the flower
of a vision on her face, the air between us
   a river of concentration.

She'll tell me to lie flat and straight, not one toe
twisted. And she'll recite the names
   of the multicoloured wolves

that howl in her head. The rain will fall
like wolf-tongues, licking my face as she talks.
   Over the sweet grass of death's field

I'll see her skeletal soul – its cartwheels
and starry spokes. She'll be wearing the Veil Nebula.
   When I talk with my mother,

my tongue will be a bud glowing in the dark.
My voice will escape in a spiral hiss.
   I'll climb down inside myself –

deeper and deeper, into the cell where words
are born, from the void and from light,
   in the universe of whirling vowels.

Descent into the Cirque de Navacelle

Come to the rim of this crater. Look down
to the bottom, to that sombre house
plunged in shadow next to the dried-up oxbow.
Consider the river that carved this amphitheatre
and you will begin to understand when I say
that's what my mother was like –
she was the River Vis, the spiral screw, the power.
She was grandiose and gripping as this view.
Take in the exposed strata. Listen as a baby might
to fossil-music. Slow your heart until you hear
the arias of ammonites. See how the seams
between an embryo's nights flex like plutonic rock.
Descend. Drive down to the pit of memory,
your body will crumble like shale as it yields.
Knock on the door of our medieval house.
If a river answers, she is my mother,
fish-scales like cymbals on her dress.
Her mouth is a blowhole, her teeth race like rapids.
Her arms were whirlpools I had to avoid.
At night, the stars washed themselves in her face.
I sat on her bed, astonished such bodies of light
could sink into her. Mealtimes were the worst,
she made me talk River. Her voice was gravel
that ground through my marrow
as she made me repeat like a grace:
"I am the Vis, the life, the strength."
Oh yes I was strong. I squeezed through fissures
in the limestone walls of my room into caves
where springs bubbled victory hymns.
I crawled up xylophone-lined tunnels
whose flood-notes poured through my body –
passages so narrow my mind was almost crushed.
My bones singing, I reached the surface.

The Limestone Madonna
in the Grotte des Demoiselles

A fall you don't seem to land from, your skull
gripped by the forceps of rushing tunnels,
through the Salle de la Main
to the massif's heart, La Cathédrale des Abîmes.
That life my mother lived in unrelieved dark
is here. She's the stalagmite Madonna –
towering, armless, white as ECT.
And that baby she's not holding
(its spine flowering from her ribs) is me.
She doesn't notice my body is a bouquet.
But she can hear the music that always played
in her head. Put an ear to the mountain
and listen to the muffled drumming,
that's how my mother speaks –
her face veiled by that stone sheet,
her mouth gagged by crystals.
Bloated by lithium, her triple chins
tremble behind its translucent folds.
Organ pipes are playing her hymns.
A million years pass, and in that slow-time
a choir of gargoyle children
rise from the floor like a fairy ring.
When they stop singing
she'll tell them her story, faster than light,
still unmarried in her mind. No man
will breach that coral-reef wedding-dress,
her cathedral of flying buttresses.
She will never remove her aisles,
the lace intricate as altar-cloths
where cave creatures are embroidered.
She is crowned by the humming halos
I could always hear during Mass –

so many stacked above her head,
giving her orders with their black voices.
And if the flame of your candle holds out,
you'll see high above her what I always saw –
her mirror-self, stalactite-sister, trying to merge,
one drip a night, until they fuse.

A Hornets' Nest

That hornets' nest was big enough
to contain two children's heads,
their paper brains
linked by tiered galleries,
the rubbish draining out of an exit hole
at the base
as Maman said it would
after the firemen came,
and we went to bed
as they released their smoke bomb.
And she smoked and talked while we drowsed,
our memories of the dog-leash and its sting
falling though the hole
at the bottom of our brains.

And here's the nest now, large as an adult's head,
the grubs preserved in their cots.
I open the pale brown envelope,
prise apart brood cells
and chew them as the hornets did once,
gnawing fibres of rotting bark into pulp,
my saliva mingling with theirs.
I taste carcasses and wings.
I flatten strips on the scorching stone wall
to dry in the afternoon of my life.
And cut my hornet-paper
into the pages of a diary.
Where now –
I remember and write everything.

The Spell

After Maman's first brainwashing session
I impaled a toad

on a thorn bush over an anthill
and watched the ants flense its flesh

until its croaks grew faint.
Then I threw the bones into the stream.

Only the key-bone floated against the current
back towards me

in a silence so deep I could hear it scream.
When that bone moored in my hand,

I repeated everything Maman had said
backwards.

The Dragonfly Daughter

The dragonfly emerges from still water,
her wings taut with surface-tension.
I know her by her French name
Libellule – meaning booklet.
She is the glass book of my childhood summers.
I stare at its covers
as if through a stained glass mosaic.
It was during those scorching siestas
that I waded upstream
deep into the underwood
and showered at the cascade,
dried my face on moss.
Afterwards, I sat on a stepping-stone
and looked into a pool
where I saw myself reflected
jewel-winged as the seraphim
from the dark pages of a child's sketchbook –
a Demoiselle with compound eyes.

So quietly did I sit, my pencil
darting its neon abdomen,
holm oaks enclosed me in an aisle.
I drew the water's wings,
the windows within windows,
the water-leaves and sun-leaves.
I felt the stream and sunlight in my veins,
the wings in my blood.
I rode the ridinghorse of my pencil's spine
up into the dazzle, where I found
Maman sleeping between the vines.
I weighed her soul with the balancing scales
of my glass horse wings.
I tangled my centaur-tail in her hair

and drove her crazy. And while
my mother took her siesta –
I sewed her lips and eyelids together
with my dragonfly needle.

The Grass Snake

I sketched the air where the grass snake
  had passed, the grassblades still quivering.

I drew my toes that had almost touched green lightning,
  that had been made new.

The fingers that drew were almost whole.
  They had never touched Maman.

For that morning spent drawing the grass snake,
  I had never been imprisoned in her body.

I arrived on earth fully-grown, on that path –
  motherless, clean.

Song Orchids

When the surgeons opened my mother
they found the rarest orchids –
the five-wounded sacred sleep
with ruby splashes on each bloom,
a blue-black hybrid like a bruise,
the dove orchid next to the flower in the form of a yellow
    serpent.

My mother's song orchids sang to me
when I crept into the operating theatre
to say goodbye to her. Without flinching
I looked at that place where I once cowered –
landing-petals shaped themselves into lips and tongues
to whisper goodbye back.

At the Gate of Secrets

after Ferenc Juhász

A mother calls out to her daughter.
Her cry climbs in a spiral.
Out of the front door she calls,
to the muscat grapes clustered like planets.
Her voice rises and keeps on rising.
It plays with the thistles
on the plateaux, and drifts
      towards the stars.

She unlooses the coil of her hair.
It falls slowly, like a universe unwinding.
Corkscrew curls tumble slow-motion
and bless her tired body.
Filaments stroke her face
like an infant's fingers.
Her grey sunken cheeks
shine in pearly moonlight
and heal for a moment.
A mother lets loose her hair
as she calls for her lost daughter.
Her auburn chevelure
swirls about her in the dusk
like a universe bursting into flower.

Her cry shakes the webs of spiders
and races icy rivers
      that scythe through rock.
Her cry overtakes the eagle ascending a thermal.
You seedheads sailing the stratosphere,
she commands, close your parachutes.
You hailstones, stop hurtling.
You migrating birds and meteor-showers,
you grids and gyres of space –
      listen to this mother's cry.

The daughter tilts her head and sniffs the air.
The velvet on her new antlers
steams in freezing solar wind
and hangs like loops
          of the Milky Way.
The points of her antlers
shine like translucent white karst
against the vaults of space.

Her mother's voice brushes galaxies
          ranged like mountains,
and echoes across the voids
          that smoke with stellar dust.
Her voice shoots through force fields
and reaches the outpost of matter.

My daughter, she calls, come back
          and take care of me.
Our limestone cottage is a ruin.
Every room awaits you.
The furniture attacks me as I pass.
Only you know how to herd the chairs
so they stop butting me with their horns.
The table legs kick me like restless colts.
Come and tame the cutlery.
It flies at me like crazed insects.
The doors slam into me like coffin lids.
When I bump into the mirror,
molten glass floods my veins
          with embalming fluid.

My eyes have been searching too long.
They glow bronze-green in their sockets
and see a thousand facets in every corner,
          like the dragonflies'.

My sight is fractured like theirs.
Each prism holds an image of you
   pulsing on my retina.

Listen – I've sewn you dresses
from threads of my memories,
in fabrics woven from my nerves.
They have the colours of my visions.
Day and night I sew
with these swollen and trembling fingers.
My hands work faster than time.
The clock winds backwards,
and your garments get smaller
until I'm making baby-lace.
And still the visions tell me to sew faster
and still you're in a filigree forest,
impaled on the thorn of my needle.
I look out through the broken window
and see the diamond-petalled stars
and you, busy in your astral garden,
tending the flowers of light
as you once nursed me, my kind daughter.

A girl pauses at the gate of secrets
and hears what she has always longed to hear.
Dear mother, she replies,
I cannot come now.
So fast did I journey through the dark,
I grew four legs.
My feet have turned to hooves.
So long did I wait for your embrace,
I lost the use of my arms.
I was naked, so my skin grew a pelt.
I do not need your clothes,
now each hair of my hide is frosted
with crystals from the stars.
My virgin womb closed.

My budding breasts shrank.
My balls swing like purses
which hold moons and suns.

My mind has sprouted a bone forest
and every bone-leaf is a shield
to protect me from your gaze.
In memory of you I grew
this crown of twin cemeteries.
Every leaf is a tombstone
carved with your name.
And every fork of my antlers
cradles a nesting nebula.

So do not call me now, my mother,
my lightning-flash antlers
would sear your womb.
My flint hooves would crack your pelvis.
The dessert grapes on your vines
would be clots of your blood
if I bit them now.
The lamps in your house would fuse
as I approached your horizon.
Mother, I cannot go back.
Your ceilings are too low.
Do not look at these synapse-trees
I carry through the night.
For my antlers soar like singing star-trees
and no human must hear them.
And I can no longer drink from my breakfast bowl
with my name painted on the side.
I must drink from the lake of pure light.

I do not understand you, my quiet
and gentle daughter. You sound
like the great stag of the oak forests.
Your voice is distorted, your words
muffled as earth on my shroud.

Even when you were home,
you hid in your tree-house.
How many times did you steal cake
and run away to the woods?
How many times did you return
and sulk in a hut of silence?
Then you'd creep upstairs
and play your flute. Every note
was a rung you could climb up.
You surrounded yourself with ladders of music.
When you finally left, the piano
punched a hole in the roof
trying to follow you. For years
the keys rained down on me.

The girl-stag listens carefully.
Her mother's voice is persistent as a cicada
on the terraces of her childhood.
Do not remind me of my home, little mother.
Everywhere I look at the hissing constellations,
I see the snakes of our derelict vineyard.
The butterfly-nebulae flitting around my horns
are suns devouring one another.
And I have not forgotten my friend
the jewelled lizard.
I have a stag's sight, and can see,
in the stellar debris,
his scales rippling with sapphire eyes.
I have a stag's nose
and can smell oxygen trickling
through the pores of antimatter.

I bleed from a billion wounds.
Every second I die.
Every second I rise back up
to run deeper into the forest,
through the root-doors
and light-rings of night,

away from your arrows, my huntress.
Sometimes your voice is so faint
I forget I am your daughter. And your voice
dips into the whirlpool
at the centre of my brain,
is sucked in and down my spine,
into my bowels
and out with my stools.

Come back, the mother begs,
you are my only daughter.
Come back from your den of splitting atoms,
  your lair of light years,
to the homely lap of your mother.
I promise to shelter you.
You do not need the star-forests.
You do not need muscles
whining like ultrasonic jets
as they pierce the locks of space.
Do not go through the gate
at the end of the garden of secrets.
I will never reach you there
with this mother's voice.

Only to die, can I return to you Mother.
Only then can you bathe me
as you did when I was a child.
Then you can scrape off my fur, my flesh.
The marrow from my bones
you can sluice with the hose.
My brittle antlers will lose their lustre
and shrivel back into my brain.
When I return, Mother, it will be
to join you in the grave
where we will torment one another.
And no one else will suffer
as you will suffer then, my mother.

Lunettes

When my father crept in, all I saw
were his glasses in the moonlight,
watching as he lifted my nightdress.
Forty years later I open the dictionary
and find *lunette*. My finger points
and I remember that's what we called them.
A little moon; spectacles;
the first semicircle of a horseshoe;
an arched aperture for the admission of light;
a crescent in a ceiling or dome
decorated with paintings or sculptures;
a blinker for a horse; a watch-glass;
in the guillotine – the hole for the victim's neck;
a flue in the side of a glass-maker's furnace
to admit smoke and flame;
a circular crystal case to hold the consecrated Host;
a linnet-hole; a forked iron plate
into which the stock of a field-gun carriage is inserted.

Oxygen

When at last the door sprang open –
what I saw was an apparition on a leash.
You had to catch your breath before embracing me.
Then I entered your tiny cluttered flat,
squeezing through a narrow path
to reach your small table. You – purse-lipped,
a hand fluttering on your heart
as if to stop it escaping,
the tubes in your nostrils, the long thin
lead which soon I'd trace
to its source: an oxygen recycling machine.
You gasped "Wait! Wait!"
I stumbled to describe my life,
you concentrated on breathing less painfully.
And when you were tired, turned the huge TV behind me
up, and looked past me at the news.
Then you slipped into bed and closed your eyes,
your back turned to me – my skeletal father.
I looked at the mustard jar half full of gold phlegm.
The oxygen machine chugged and hummed,
its rhythm shaking the floor like a ship's engine.
It rose through the soles of my feet, through the table,
into my palms and elbows, through the chair legs
into the seat and my sex –
that surge and hiss, pump and release,
speaking to me through the core of my bones.
The machine that drives the lost world
where I'm still waiting, even now. As long
as I can remember that sound
with every fibre of my body, you are still breathing.

The Orchid Hunter

Each morning I am an orchid hunter.
I need to find the flowers
triggered by rains,
to circle the lake
and pick from its overhanging branches
        the large oculatas
shaped like grinning masks,
the little bulls of Moctezuma's gardens,
the serpenthead, the tiger, the nun,
        the devil's horns,
the black-flower, fall-blooming, flower of the dead,
the partially open vanilla orchid vines
        fresh from the Florentine Codex.
Their petals are the skin of god.
I need their skirt-lips, their erect,
        arching, single-valved clams,
and the triangular blossoms so small
only a glass can find them,
their fragrant green faces with chocolate veins
        and a braid of leaves,
the dark blue buds glistening in the crotch
        of a tree,
deep in the forests of El Paraíso State.

Noon in the Orchid House, Kew Gardens

Didn't I tell you you're my Prince of Flowers?
I've come to Kew. I'm kissing each bloom
until one kisses back, bites like you.
I'm drifting to the Isla de Sacrificios.
It smells of vanilla, drips with steam.
I can see through the green and glass haze
into Sonora, into the hottest hour.
Of course, when I find you, you're an orchid,
clinging to the porous roof of a host.
Your testicular roots dangle in my skull.

The Mirror Orchid

A megasaurian massif reared above our vineyard,
its reptile-scale thistles slowly opening and closing during
                              siestas as if they wanted to speak.

Since childhood I looked up, wanting to walk for weeks
                              undisturbed on the spiny crest
        of the great garrigue,
my catching-flies-mouth open, my eyes half-closed, chasing
        the glimpsed tail of a crystalline beast in the blur of my
                              flickering eyelashes.

Even down in the terraces, among the vines, dragonflies with
                              quartz wings and meteor eyes
brought the perfume of the plateau – a cloud I could vanish in if
                              I dared.

And now here I am climbing the giant stone ladder –
its rungs wide as the horizon, my knuckles grazed by falling
                              rocks.
Each gap a viridian-rivered gorge where I bathe and shed the
                              twelve scare-skins of singlehood.

Until at last I arrive with my magnifying glass, parting the
                              straw-grasses,
the golden sword-leafed thistle-heads like desert medusas, the
                              fossil-flowers with stone petals
        and sulphur stems.

Iridescent-black horned beetles crawl out of their corollas and
                              wave antennae at me,
        bearing news from subterranean voyages.
What ultraviolet jewels have they seen? What silences have they
                              plumbed,
        to surface in roaring whirlpools of sunlight?
And the mistral blasting their armour-plates, as they scuttle out,
                              gilded with pollen,

some with arrows on their backs, pointing – This way! Urgent!
                                                          Urgent!
So I follow the trilobite tribe. I trust them.
I walk until my feet are numb, so numb they glide like
                              millipedes across millennia.

They lead me to a blue light beckoning on a stem – a tiny,
                                        speckled speculum.
The queen of subterfuge, a wasp-orchid with a looking-glass sex.

All the sky's pigment is packed in this sky-swallower, this
                                              plasma screen
where time unreels, frame by frame, as I inch nearer, my face
                              gripped by the cave of its calyx,

where even stalactite-seconds have stopped dripping.
Where a prehistoric cicada sings a stone song – a clock-tick my
                              ears must tune themselves to.

In the upside-down sky of its pheromone-trap, a scent-song is
                                                    released
        for only one lover.
I enter the central crystal nest, star-factory, world-window, nadir
where stem-tunnels draw me down through etiolated systems of
                                                          roots.

I drink the sap of solitude, scalding as magma, heavy as the iron
                              core of my planet.

Ophrys miroir is vibrating now, metamorphosing into a female
                                                          wasp,
passing through incandescent larva stages. Her blue wings
                                                  shimmer
like the vernix on a newborn baby. Like the flawless lens on a
                              newly cast telescope.

And now, before I drown in light, I must peer into the stinging
                                        heart of the Larzac
where the fire-petalled flowers of the void sway.
I greet the toothed flowers of sleep and their pollinators.
I greet their silent, long, thorned, spiral stems, their
                                        planet-sucking roots.

Through black veils of night's nucleus, the sky-insects come.
The midnight scarab, the blood-spitter, the great Capricorn and
                                        flying stag –
all the burying beetles of my lonely life.

And the orb-spider whose web is an island galaxy –
my swaddled, half-digested dreams dangle from the zigzag that
                                        streaks her net.

Mirror of Venus glistens, her stamens poised above me
like hammers or brushes that will repaint me if I don't run.

A wasp, or a lover? Conjured from the long cobalt corridors
                                        under the petal,
I hear him approach, his wings humming with nervous light.

Networks of sunrays harnessed for his flight to the mirror-
                                        flower, whose petals
are opening for me like the sheets of a plush azure bed,
the velvet nap lithe with solar flares but cool to my touch.

Again and again, the pollinia are stuck to my head as I tumble
                                        into their gold thunders.

And my lover clasps me, drawing close as a male wasp can
                                        draw to a flower –
        alien species to alien species.

House of Solitude

A deep hum like a swarm in the corner of the room,
then a roar like a jet engine as if my house is taking off.
My sight grows sharp as a microscope – the longer
I go without seeing anyone, the higher its power.
If a fortnight passes and I haven't gone out,
the clocks unfurl like flowers. The minutes are moths
settling on my hand – their wings alight with feathery flames.
I can see inside light, to the shadows behind atoms
where silence makes its nests – as many silences as there are
    birds.
Each has a song that only I can hear.
The stars come close then, leaning their faces against my
    window
like parents who have incarcerated their child,
who say one word through the glass. One word
like a nightly diet – by which I have to live.

Carving the Dead Elm of Le Caylar

The Larzac, a country of 'story solitude' – Paul Marres

I like to start before dawn, when the bark is still coursing with
                                        star-sap,
when I can see filaments of oxygen pour through glass leaves of
                                        the ghost-canopy,
    before the sun evaporates them.

My carved creatures talk with root tongues.
They tell me their story solitudes,
and I try to be true to them, I who have not spent my life at the
                        heart of this huge plateau,

but who can draw from the well of my soul, as from tree rings,
                        the concentric solitudes.
I release them with my mallet, in the fading moon's balm.

I draw up the toad, the cops owl, the ram, the giant carline
                                        thistle
    opening at first light like a supernova.

I summon the bison beetle, the wild boar, the royal eagle.
They pass through the conduits of my arms and out through my
                                        fingers.

The chisel's nose smells their fears as it strokes their skins.

I work fast, before noise taints the day, attending to the silences
streaming in from the Grand Larzac Causse,
                that gather around this elm like an axis.

My armoire, ormeau mort, engraved with an acorn from the
                                pubescent white oak,
a hornets' nest, a horn of plenty, an ear of wheat – all wood-
                                        quiet.

These are the forms I can name. Others my chisel shapes when
                                                    I'm tired. Then
it's as if the Larzac is working through me,
carving the mistral's masks, the night's pageant.

And the shepherd who has seen these things.
As the sun rises, the lamb he is carrying across his shoulders
                                                    grows heavy
        as a dead tree.

He whispers this to me, from his place in the lower trunk, when
                                        I am too exhausted to go on.
My body lightens then. I climb to the top of the main branch

and carve a pilot hanging naked, his feet caught by snakes, his
                                                    arms raised
as if trailing an invisible parachute,
            its silks tangled in boughs of the Milky Way.

The Door Flower

The Caussenards pin huge carline thistles
on their front doors to tell the weather

A giant carline thistle flowerhead was pinned to our cottage
                                                                    door
   like the Cartwheel Galaxy.
It told us the weather, its calyx a resurrection of anther-flames.

Sunshine opened the door's petals –
our home was fertilised by insects of light.

Our chairs turned hermaphrodite
and could self-pollinate and multiply to seat ghost visitors.

Bread materialised, as if from bakeries in the table-legs' taproots,
baked in the ovens at our planet's core – hot bread
that even skeletons could eat
            and the flesh would rise like yeast.

But cloud closed the straw-gold rays.
            Before rain,
the thistle's rosette of thorns swelled shut, let no chink in –
not even a keyhole, should the sun shrink itself
to a firekey
       and prise the plant of night.

While veils of falling rain-blossom enveloped our roof,

we sat around the hurricane lamp reading legends
of the Larzac. Behind each page of lightning-print
a fossil lizard basked.

Prehistoric portal,
           garlanded with iron canopy of spectral vines,
shaded by the figtree and its hornet hum.
Haunted by a Montpellier snake – himself a surge
     of flashing firedoors –

door carved from all the woods of the forest,
                              even the August blaze.
Sky door conjured from dragonfly-wing shimmer,
      flying door-tree.

Now shrouded under swags of dusty spider webs.

Rough door that I used to hug – those childhood dawns –
before leaving our fragrant vineyard with its ecstatic cicadas
to climb onto the Causse Noir.
                              Waiting for stemless carlines
to burst from the rock like dinosaur eyes.

I stared at those chthonic flowers until I disappeared
down spiral traps with ultraviolet honeyguides.

I tumbled into the felt gorges between stamen and stigma.
And deep in the carline's corolla
I smelt the prickly perfume of our door.
And it was near as a thunder electron,
                              and far as the Horsehead Nebula.

Spiny leaf-door that used to creak open at the beginning of
                                        summer.
Volted voicebox –
from which came the sigh flowers make, as the bee
            brushes against their lips.

Barricaded door, painted with a skull and crossbones,
that I have to force, moth-blinded, drinking night's nectar.

Our double-door that admitted a donkey and cart
                              laden with the grape harvest.
And us on our sleeping-platform, exhausted and heat-struck,

sifting through seed-stars in their black husks.
Our door-flower guarding the deepest dreams in sleep's vat.

I lay with my head under the broken chimney, watching pollen
        drift down from the high meadows of the universe
to gild my pillow.

Unearthly Languages

I was fluent in the music of the spheres
but it faded. So I salvaged one note

and kept it under my tongue
to fuel my first breath.

After my birth, I broke that note into colours
with which to see the world –

our home, where I was locked
in the cellar of myself.

The door has a leash hanging from it,
with little bells that shiver,

the way frost tinkles on a starry night.
Then the door clicks open and I go out

and stand naked
while snowflakes melt on my skin,

like the words of a lost language.

A Piano Flower

The black keys of night and the white keys of day are in
          harmony for a moment,
if we are quiet enough to hear them,

and brave enough to go down the long vibrating pathways
          between atoms,
where anthers are felt hammers

in the corolla cabinet
and galaxies of pollen notes explode on our eardrums.

If we dare look at music's sound-palette,
and see nuclei dance to Ur-colours,

if we could stroke, with fingers of light,
the root of a mountain, the breath of a bird,

the constellation of a wolf-howl through the void,
if we could accompany each other down those shivery
          corridors

and play a duet on the piano flower
so as to summon the stars from their holes,

we'd play a nocturne that could lift
our own flowers up through our bones and out through our
          fingers

like a fragrance on the keyboard –
how we could live then, listening to each other.

Acknowledgements

Many thanks to the editors of the following, in which some of these poems first appeared: *Antología Letras en el Golfo* (Mexico), *Boomerang, The Forward Book of Poetry 2005, Free Verse, Magma, The Manhattan Review, Modern Poetry in Translation, Poetry International, Poetry Wales, The Pterodactyl's Wing, Quadrant, Quattrocento* and *The Rialto*.

'Noon in the Orchid House, Kew Gardens' was commissioned for National Poetry Day and broadcast on BBC Radio 4. 'A Piano Flower' was commissioned for *Plant Care: A Festschrift for Mimi Khalvati*. 'At the Gate of Secrets' is indebted to Kenneth McRobbie's and Ted Hughes' translations of Ferenc Juhász' 'The Boy Changed into a Stag Cries Out at the Gate of Secrets'.

I am extremely grateful to the Royal Literary Fund for generous financial support to finish this book.